Let's Read About Pets

Goldfish

JoAnn Early Macken

Reading consultant: Susan Nations

W
FRANKLIN WATTS
LONDON • SYDNEY

First UK hardback edition 2004
First UK paperback edition 2005

Franklin Watts
96 Leonard Street
London EC2A 4XD

Franklin Watts Australia
45-51 Huntley Street
Alexandria
NSW 2015

ISBN 0 7496 5762 6 (hardback)
ISBN 0 7496 5829 0 (paperback)

Published in association with Weekly Reader Early Learning Library, Milwaukee.

Printed in Hong Kong, China

Contents

Colours

Not all goldfish are gold. They may be black, red, white or other colours.

A scaly skin

Goldfish may have spots, stripes or other patterns on their bodies. Their bodies are covered with **scales**.

scales

Fast swimmers

Some goldfish have slim bodies and long, slender tail **fins**. These fish can swim fast through the water.

fins

Slow swimmers

Some goldfish have thick bodies and large, rounded tail fins. These fish cannot swim very fast.

How goldfish breathe

Goldfish breathe with **gills**. Gills take oxygen from the water.

gills

Your fish tank

To keep goldfish, you need an aquarium, or tank. It is important to keep the tank clean.

Hiding places

Goldfish like to hide. Give your fish places where it can hide. Put rocks, plants and ornaments in your tank.

Sleep

Goldfish cannot close their eyes. When they sleep, they sink to the bottom of the tank and stay still.

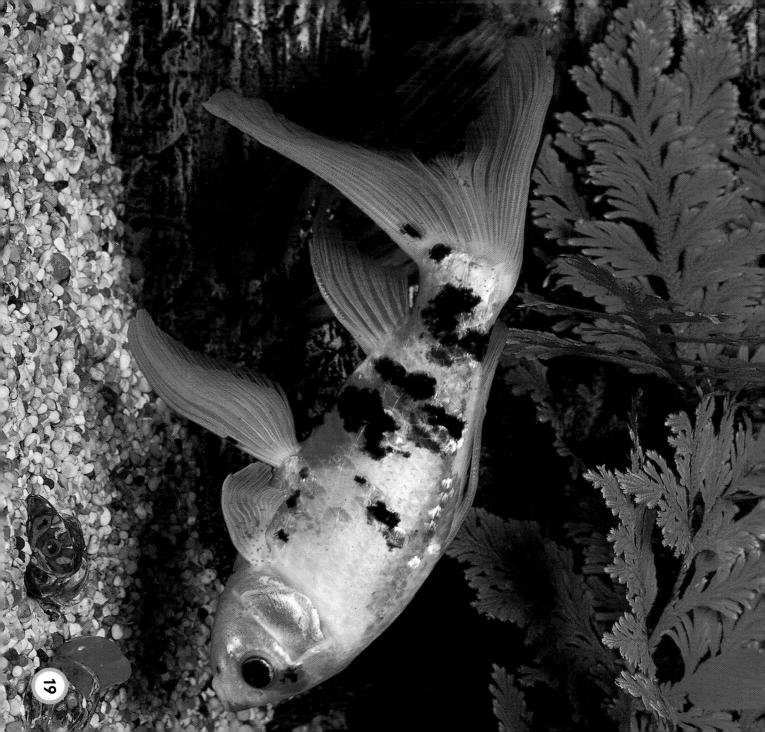

Feeding your fish

Goldfish need the right food to stay healthy. Feed them with goldfish food flakes twice a day. Take care not to give them too much!

New words

gills – the parts of the fish that allow it to breathe in the water

ornaments – objects used to decorate something

oxygen – a gas in the air that people and animals breathe

patterns – designs

slender – not fat

How to find out more

Here are some useful websites about goldfish:

www.bbc.co.uk/cbbc/wild/pets
Factsheets on goldfish and other pets, including an interactive guide on a goldfish's behaviour

www.ispca.ie/petcare/pet-goldfish.html
Tips on what a goldfish needs

www.bbc.co.uk/tees/features/animals/fish
Click on the photo to discover the names of the different parts of a goldfish, plus tips on keeping fish

www.abc.net.au/creaturefeatures/facts/fish.htm
Useful facts about goldfish

Note We strongly advise that Internet access is supervised by a responsible adult.